What Readers Are Saying...

"Once again, Janet McBride has hit the mark with her ability to apply ancient mysteries to our modern methods. The miracles of God's creation are vast and relevant in ways beyond the paradigms of religion; and simply because a different culture preserved those mysteries and applies them for health and prosperity, the question we should ask is not whether they are pagan, but are they validated through the Word of God.

It's hard to imagine trying to walk on water, even with Jesus reaching out to Peter outside the boat. But the reality is, just because we think something cannot be done does not mean our beliefs are correct. *Feng Shui, God's Way* proves once again that those who seek truth and wisdom from God will receive it according to His Will and perhaps in ways we may not comprehend. But that in itself proves that God's Creation is the same no matter how it is packaged."

~ Ken Schortgen, Jr., Author
"The Day No Man Knows"
www.GodsProfessor.com

"Janet McBride has written a wonderful combination of a fascinating exploration into the origins of *Feng Shui,* joined with the practical steps to use these timeless principles to enhance your life."

~ Ellen S. Rogin, CPA, CFP®
Author, *Great with Money: The Women's Guide to Prosperity*
www.sfd-inc.com
www.begreatwithmoney.com

"I love connecting to another layer of *Feng Shui.* I believe this book will bridge the mystical with the spiritual for many people who appreciate the Bible's teachings and have wondered how these universal teachings fit with "God's Way."

There is a spiritual connection to everything in this world, and I enjoyed how Janet has applied this to *Feng Shui.* She has very eloquently shown us that *Feng Shui* is not just a Chinese philosophy, but a Universal truth."

~ Shauna Piscitello
Living in Balance with Feng Shui™
www.livinginbalance.org

Feng Shui 風水 God's Way

The Secret Was Here
All the Time

Janet McBride

*""God understands the way of Wisdom, and He knows its place,
for He looks to the ends of the Earth and sees under the whole
Heavens to establish a weight for the **Wind** (**Feng**),
and apportions **Water** (**Shui**) by His measure."*

~ Job 28:23-25 ~

Cedar Hill Publishing

Cover design by Rebecca Hayes

Book design by Rebecca Hayes

Published in the United States by
Cedar Hill Publishing
Snowflake, AZ 85937
www.cedarhillpublishing.com

ISBN-13: 978-0-9816919-4-7

Library of Congress Control Number 2008926894

With sincere gratitude and thanksgiving,
I dedicate this work to the Author of
the Universal Law of Wind and Water.
He is the Tao; the Beginning and the End;
the Alpha and Omega;
the One Who knows me best
… Yeshua ha Mashiach.

Acknowledgments

Joe McBride - My forever love and deepest gratitude to you— the *"one who makes me better than I am alone."* I'm grateful for your patience and support through this amazing project; for supporting and financing my trips to *Feng Shui* school; and for 32 years of unconditional love … This one's for you, Joe.

Terah Kathryn Collins - My knowledge, appreciation and passion for the *Art of Feng Shui* would not be possible without your influence and commitment. You are a brilliant mentor and intuitive Master of *Feng Shui*, and I am privileged to have been your student. Thank you for touching the lives of so many at the *Western School of Feng Shui.*

Ellen Rogin – It hardly seems like 8 years have passed since our lives crossed forever at *Feng Shui* school. I am grateful to G-d for the connection we made that summer, which has developed into a beautiful friendship. You epitomize the legendary *Virtuous Woman* that King Solomon esteemed in Proverbs 31. I am truly blessed to call you "friend."

Shauna Piscitello – Over the years since we graduated the *Western School of Feng Shui,* I've witnessed your tremendous success as a *Feng Shui* professional, while balancing your other roles as wife and mother equally well. It must be that you truly walk the talk when it comes to *Feng Shui.* You are undeniably a woman that others should emulate. Thank you for your friendship and support.

Becky Hayes – We made it through one more go-around of edits; typesetting; graphics placement; and endless rewrites. Thanks for being brilliant at what you do and patient with my never-ending changes. You're a true Pro!

Table of Contents

About the Author
Janet McBride

Feng Shui Practitioner, Author, Radio Talk Show Personality, Ordained Minister, Business Owner and Messianic Psalmist.

Janet McBride became interested in the subject of Feng Shui by "Divine Synchronicity." She believes her steps are ordained and "when the student is ready, the teacher will appear." In this case, it was world-renowned teacher and author Terah Kathryn Collins.

Following her graduation from the Western School of Feng Shui in San Diego, California, Janet's journey took her back to her Hebraic Roots in the ancient Scriptures. From there, the grand design of *Feng Shui God's Way* began to emerge.

Janet McBride's achievements are showcased in *Who's Who in American Women 2002-2008.* In addition to her published works and Health BLOG, Janet lectures in Churches, Community Groups and recently hosted her own Detroit Radio Health Show. She has also appeared on numerous other radio programs including CNN News.com and was featured on the Television Program "The Opportunity Show" with Robin Seymour.

Janet McBride resides with her family in the beautiful White Mountains of Arizona. She is the mother of 4 and grandmother of 5, and pursues her passion of empowering women to create wealth by working from home.

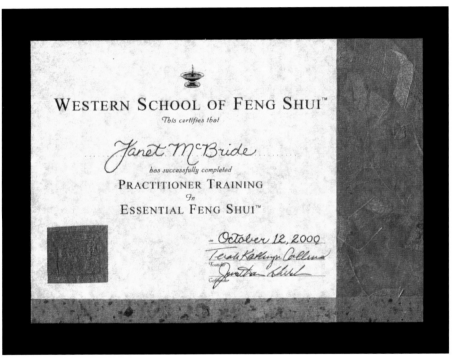

WESTERN SCHOOL OF FENG SHUI™

This certifies that

Janet McBride

has successfully completed

PRACTITIONER TRAINING

In

ESSENTIAL FENG SHUI™

on October 12, 2000

Preface

Over the past two decades, the practice of *Feng Shui* has gained popularity in Western Culture. But the Secrets of *Feng Shui* are as ancient as the Garden of Eden. *Feng Shui* (pronounced phonetically as Fung Schway) refers to the planned design in which we arrange our environment to enhance our lifestyles. Is it really possible to improve lives by simply rearranging furniture or clearing clutter? Many people think so! But *Feng Shui* is so much more than mere placement and design. It's one of the immutable Natural Laws of the Universe, instituted by God at the time of Creation.

The term *Feng Shui* is Chinese and translates to "Wind and Water." These are the two elements in Nature, which by their movement, affect change in all the other elements. Wind and Water are also, according to ancient Scriptures, two manifestations of the God's Spirit:

*"And suddenly there came a sound from Heaven as of a rushing mighty **Wind**... and they were all filled with the **Holy Spirit**."*
~ Acts 2:2 and 4

*"The **Spirit of God** Vibrated Over the Face of the **Waters**."*
~ Genesis 1:2

Within these texts we see that the Spirit of God is vibrating in all of Creation. Through this understanding of Nature's vibrational frequency, we can choose to work in concert with God's Natural Laws to enhance our lifestyles, our health and our finances.

It is a generally accepted belief that the Chinese culture is responsible for preserving the principles and the practice of *Feng Shui*. And, it is with the greatest respect and appreciation for these beliefs and principles handed down from a time-honored people that I put forth for your consideration the evidence that *Feng Shui* does not originate with the Chinese, but can be traced all the way back to Genesis... *In the Beginning*.

You are about to embark on a journey to uncover truths buried beneath millennia of superstition and skepticism concerning the practice of *Feng Shui*. Through the Hebraic Roots of the *Torah* and other ancient writings, you will discover that as with all of God's Natural Laws, the Law of Wind and Water is a gift from the Creator to His children. *Feng Shui God's Way* is intended to open a window to the eyes of your understanding, because ***the Secret was here all the time***.

Introduction

The journey to discover **Feng Shui God's Way** begins with simple instructions. Historically, these instructions or *Torah* (Hebrew for the "Instructions") were first imparted to Adam; then later to Job; and down through the portals of time to the great patriarchs, Abraham, Isaac and Jacob; and finally recorded by the prophet Moses to empower God's creation concerning every aspect of life on Planet Earth. And while God's immutable, natural laws have existed since time immemorial, they are first truly observed in action in the story of Noah (3,000 B.C.E.). Is it mere coincidence that most *Feng Shui* scholars agree the Chinese practice of *Feng Shui* dates to 3,000 B.C.E. as well? It is this author's belief that the origin of *Feng Shui* began at the moment when *"... God created the Heavens and the Earth."* (Genesis 1:1)

So how did the practice become associated primarily with the Chinese culture? To uncover these and other mysteries, we must journey back in time and place to an historic event that changed the global village we call Earth, forever. The time? 2,000 B.C.E. The place? The Tower of Babel, which is modern day Iraq. The events leading up to the building of the Tower and the great scattering of peoples and languages that followed as recorded in the Book of Genesis, set the stage for the Chinese people to adopt the Law of Wind and Water as their own.

No one seems to know why the practice is called wind and water; however, according to one author (Richard Webster), *Feng Shui* is a relatively new term. The Chinese characters for *Feng Shui* in more ancient times were "Ham and Yu." In the Hebrew language, *Feng Shui* is translated as *Ruach Mayim* (wind and water). The popularity of *Feng Shui* in the western world gained prominence at the end of the 20th Century.

As King Solomon wrote, *"Of the making of many books there is*

1

no end..." (Eccles. 12:12b) This can be said of the subject of *Feng Shui.* I write this one more book to challenge believers in the traditional Holy Scriptures who might otherwise discount the principles of *Feng Shui* as mere superstition and occultism. And equally, I challenge the New Age thinkers to consider an alternative origin for this highly favored practice of the Ancients. I ask that you, the reader, keep an open mind as you journey with me into the past to find answers to our present-day struggles. To glean and understand the value of this information, it will require that you allow the Holy Spirit to break down your paradigms and prejudices of what others may have told you about *Feng Shui.* Return to *Source* for truth. His promise to you is that *"You shall know the truth, and the truth shall make you free."* (John 8:32)

The instructions for Planet Earth are the same for everyone; and once these instructions are revealed in the light of their spiritual birthplace, it is my hope that each person who journeys with me will freely and without confusion or religious encumbrances, experience a life of peace and joy through the blessing of **Feng Shui, God's Way.**

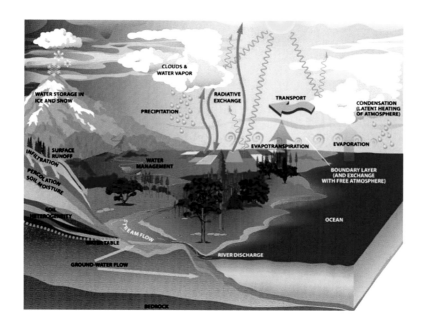

THE LAW OF WIND AND WATER

*"The wind (Feng) goes toward the South (Fire) and turns
around to the North (Water). The wind whirls about
continually and comes again on its circuit. All the rivers
run into the sea, and yet the sea is not full. To the place
from which the rivers come, there they return again."*
~ Ecclesiastes 1:6-7

Part 1 –
The Biblical Roots of Feng Shui

Chapter 1 –
In the Beginning

"In the Beginning, God Created the Heavens and the Earth." (Genesis 1:1) The **Earth** element is the first of the five elements of *Feng Shui* to be manifest in the story of Creation. And then *"The Spirit of God vibrated over the face of the waters."* (**Water** Element) The Hebrew word for "Spirit" in this text is *Ruach* and is the same as the Hebrew word for "Wind." And so herein we discover the origin of *Feng Shui,* the Law of "Wind and Water." In the beginning, God introduced the elements of *Feng Shui* into the whole of Creation by His Spirit when He created the Heavens and the Earth, and the "Wind" of His Spirit vibrated over the face the "Waters." (Genesis 1:2)

After the **Water** element began to vibrate with a Heavenly frequency, a new element took form—the element of **Fire.** For God then spoke the words: *"Let there be Light and there was Light."* (Gen 1:3) Light is a powerful source of energy and works in concert with the other elements of *Feng Shui* to create a healthy flow of *Ch'i* throughout our environment. *Ch'i* is the Chinese word for "life force" or the "breath of life" which is the measurable flow of energy found in Nature. The element of **Fire** was created in two forms: the Sun, which is the greater light by day, and the Moon, which is the lesser light by night. These represent the Fire Elements in creation and each has its place of importance in the natural Law of Opposites: Night and Day; Dark and Light; Sun and Moon. Conventional *Feng Shui* refers to this Law of Opposites as *Yin and Yang.*

After Earth, Wind, Fire and Water, the next element of *Feng Shui* to appear in creation was the **Wood** element: *"Then God said, "Let the Earth bring forth **grass**, the **herbs** and the **fruit trees**…"* ~ Gen. 1:11

And finally, the element of **Metal** came forth as a symbol of rich land in Eden: *"And the **Gold** of that land is good…and the **Onyx** stone is there."* ~ Gen. 2:12

All of the elements of *Feng Shui* are encompassed in the Genesis story of Creation: Earth, Water, Fire, Wood, Metal and the Wind of God's Spirit that governs them all. These environmental elements are the quintessential factors of *Feng Shui*. According to Terah Kathryn Collins, author and founder of the *Western School of Feng Shui*, these five are considered *"the building blocks of everything physical on the Planet." (Western Guide to Feng Shui)*

The sixth element of Wind represents the Spirit of the Creator and the Natural *Ch'i* or Life Force that overshadows and gives wings to nature's building blocks. Introducing and controlling the natural elements into each living space can achieve harmony and balance. ***Feng Shui God's Way*'s** perspective of these elements from ancient Biblical writings illustrates the patterns God employs to nourish and control their natural cycles.

The elements of *Feng Shui* were clearly at work bringing the entire creation into perfect harmony and balance. *Torah* says the Creator *looked at what He had made and saw that it was good.* He instituted the natural order of life on Planet Earth, and indeed it was very good. (Genesis 1:31)

The highest of all creations, Man, was formed from the element of **Earth**. Man was called *"Male and Female,"* hence we coined the words "Mankind" and "Humanity." The man and the woman were placed in the Garden of Delight (*Gan Eden*) where the climate was so perfect that all things grew in abundance. Every herb, every blade of grass was whole and nutritionally rich for food. Nature was at her perfection. Richard Webster, *Feng Shui* consultant and international speaker writes: *"Ch'i is the universal life force which gathers near gently flowing water and is created whenever anything is done perfectly."* (*101 Feng Shui Tips for the Home*) When the Universal Natural Law of *Feng Shui* is allowed to govern, the environment is perfectly harmonized.

In the center of this Garden of Delight grew the source for immortality, the **Tree of Life**. But God prevented the original man and woman from accessing the Tree of Life because they had violated His commandment to refrain from accessing the other tree in the Garden — the **Tree of the Knowledge of Good and Evil.** Because of their disobedience, the end of  every living thing on the Earth was set into motion. Each person would have an appointed time when the "breath of life" *(Ch'i)* would depart. However, in His mercy and grace, God promised to restore the **Tree of Life** at the end of time when His Heavenly Kingdom is established on Planet Earth. (Revelation 22:1-2)

And so, until each appointed time, the natural flow of Wind and Water; Seedtime and Harvest; and the Breath of Life itself will continue on the Earth for all creation to experience and enjoy.

Chapter 2 –
The Natural Cycles of
Feng Shui

The expression of the five elements in *Torah* — Earth, Fire, Water, Wood and Metal – gives us an understanding of God's interaction with His creation, just as the Chinese principles of *Feng Shui* teach the *Productive* and the *Destructive* Cycles of these five elements. For example, in the *Productive* Cycle, Wood feeds a Fire, and Fire produces Ash or the Earth element. The ancient Hebraic practice of burnt offerings was man's expression of thanksgiving, repentance or obedience toward God. The **Wood** was consumed along with the **Fire** of the sacrificial offering, producing **Earth**. This type of offering activated the *Productive* Cycle of forgiveness and blessing because it was well-pleasing to God. Following his deliverance from the flood, Noah offered a burnt sacrifice to his God. The Scriptures record that because of this favorable offering, God promised to never again curse the Earth with floodwaters. (Genesis 9:11)

The flood came because a *Destructive* Cycle in nature was set in motion through man's flagrant violation of God's laws. The violations triggered an imbalance that weakened the *ch'i* or life-giving energy on the Earth. As the Noahic Record indicates, when harmony and order give way to discord and chaos, the path to restoration of the natural order must first come through the *Destructive* Cycle of *Feng Shui*. God purged the Earth of *shar ch'i* (evil) by means of a worldwide flood:

"And behold, I Myself (God), am bringing floodwaters on the earth to destroy all that has the breath of life (ch'i)... because the heart of man is on evil continually."
~ *Genesis 6:5, 17*

The Five Elements

Productive Cycle   **Domination Cycle**

Through this *Destructive* or *Domination* Cycle, the chaos was abated and the way was made clear to begin the restoration process. And through it all, God preserved a healthy remnant of His creation on-board the confines of the Ark. When the waters receded and it was time to restore the healthy flow of *ch'i* to the Earth, Noah initiated the *Productive* Cycle by offering the burnt sacrifice to the Creator of Heaven and Earth. His efforts were greatly rewarded in that God set a Rainbow in the Heavens, a manifestation of healing light and color never before seen on the Earth. And with the Rainbow, He made His covenant promise never to send the floodwaters again. (Genesis 8:21)

Feng Shui God's Way played a significant role in the story of Noah's Ark because it was through the elements of "Wind and Water" and the *Productive and Destructive Cycles* of Nature that God removed all unrighteousness from Earth and started the process anew:

*"God made a wind (**Feng**) to pass over the earth, and the waters (**Shui**) subsided."* ~ *Genesis 8:1*

Chapter 3 –
Opposites Attract

After the Great Flood, another universal law was revealed: The Law of Polarity or *Opposites*. This is also known as the Law of *Yin and Yang* and represents the polar opposites in nature that work in harmony to create a complete and balanced cycle. The Law of Opposites says that if there is an "up," there must be a "down." If there is a "right," there must be a "left." Or if there is a "back," there must also be a "front."

Vocabulary experts define the concept of **yin** and **yang** as two opposing and, at the same time, complementary aspects of any one object, process or comparison. They are universal standards of quality. (Wikipedia) In keeping with the simplicity of **Feng Shui God's Way**, our ancient guidebook beautifully describes the Law of Opposites as a perpetual and predictable phenomenon within the Creation:

*"And God said to Noah, 'While the Earth remains, there shall be Seedtime and Harvest (**yin and yang**); Cold and Heat (**yin and yang**); Winter and Summer (**yin and yang**); and Day and Night (**yin and yang**) shall not cease."*
~ Genesis 8:22

The cycles of life are created by the never-ending flow of *yin and yang*: Day follows into night, and night into the following day. Seasons follow seasons; sunrise and sunset. This is how we mark time and why we age. With each passing cycle, we should seize the moments; breathe-in the goodness of all that God has given, cherish the days of our youth, and embrace the years of our experience and learning. Wisdom is not given to the younger, but is reserved for those who have earned it… *"Wisdom is the gray hair unto men and women, and an unspotted life is old age."* (Wisdom of Solomon 4:9)

If we are faithful to follow God's natural laws and respect all that He has created, we can expect to receive the blessing of a long and prosperous life on Earth until the *appointed time.*

Chapter 4 –
The Mouth of Ch'i

Now that you've observed how the Law of Wind and Water affected the lives of Noah, his family and the whole Earth, let's move forward through history to a time when the Nation of Israel was enslaved in the land of Egypt. The time is approximately 1,500 B.C.E. God saved a child from the wrath of Pharaoh by means of *"wind and water"* only to eventually bring him face to face in conflict against the Egyptian royal family who raised him.

The child was first carried on the *waters* of the Nile River by the *wind* and rescued by Pharaoh's Daughter. The child grew to become the Deliverer Moses. On the eve of Israel's deliverance from 400 years of slavery, God instructed Moses to direct each Hebrew family to cover the doorpost and lintels of the **front entrance** to their homes with the blood of the Passover lamb.

*"And you shall take a bunch of hyssop, dip it in the blood...and
strike the lintel and the two doorposts with the lamb's blood.
And none of you shall go out of his house until morning."
~ Exodus 12:22*

Feng Shui operates on the premise that *ch'i*, God's natural energy, enters a house or building through the **front entrance**. This is called the *"Mouth of Ch'i."* Because God was sending a *Destructive Cycle* of Energy or negative *ch'i* to settle the account with Pharaoh, it was necessary that the Israelites take immediate action to deflect this negative energy from coming into their own homes. *Feng Shui God's Way* was achieved through the application of the blood of the Passover lamb over the *mouth of ch'i,* the front entrance.

Additionally, in the practice of *Feng Shui,* the color **"Red"** is very auspicious and believed to have a powerful energetic effect on the environment. It was certainly true in the story of the Passover, for when the "Destroyer" *(Destructive Cycle)* passed through, the first-born of every Egyptian household, including Pharaoh's was stricken. But the firstborn of the Nation of Israel, whose **front entrances** were covered with the auspicious **Red** blood of the Passover lamb, were delivered.

"For the Lord will pass through to strike the Egyptians;
And when He sees the blood on the lintel and on the two doorposts,
The Lord will pass over the door and not allow the Destroyer to come into your houses to strike you." ~ Exodus 12:23

The events that led to the destruction of Pharaoh and ultimately to all of Egypt that day were the fruits of Natural Laws: Sowing and Reaping, combined with the Law of *Feng Shui*. Pharaoh sowed seeds of murder in his heart, intending to kill the firstborn of Israel. As a result, God turned the tables and instructed the Israelites to employ *Feng Shui* to protect the

Mouth of Ch'i with the auspicious **Red** blood of the Passover lamb. Egypt suffered because of the hatred in Pharaoh's heart, and the whole nation became the victim of his curse.

> *"Do not be deceived. God is not mocked; for whatever*
> *a man sows, that he will also reap." ~ Galatians 6:7*

Chapter 5 –
Feng Shui, the Art of Divine Design

When Israel was at last released from the bondage of Egypt, God ordained the establishment of the Tabernacle in the Wilderness. *Torah* tells us that God gave specific instructions to Moses at Mount Sinai for the creation of this tent-like structure:

*"Then the Lord spoke to Moses, saying...'You shall set up the tabernacle of the tent of meeting...you shall partition off the ark (of the covenant) with the veil... You shall bring in the table and **arrange the things** that are to be **set in order** on it; and you shall bring in the Menorah and light its lamps. You shall set the altar **before** the door of the Tabernacle (Mouth of Ch'i); you shall set the laver (water) **between** the Tabernacle and the altar... Moses put the table **on** the North side of the Tabernacle...and he put the Menorah **across** from the table on the **South** side of the Tabernacle and lit the lamps (fire).'"*
~ Exodus 40:2-24

Among the many *Feng Shui* applications noted in these passages, it's interesting to observe that God was very specific about the placement of each piece of furniture. Placement is very important in the practice of *Feng Shui*. You can open the space around you to free-flowing *ch'i* and greater blessing, or you can stagnate the flow of the Creator's breath of life by poor placement or misalignment of the items in your home. It's also interesting to note that the table on which all the items were to be arranged was to be oriented to the **North** side of the Tabernacle, while the Menorah, the holder of fire and lights, was to be located on the **South** side.

21

The Law of Wind and Water teaches that the direction of **North** is the most powerful direction. *Feng Shui* author Penelope Lindsay, writes:

*"From the Chinese point of view, in Earth's northern hemisphere, the pivot point of the heavens is the North Star or Polaris…Polaris symbolizes the beginning of order, hence the use of **North** as the focus for orienting the Bagua grid…"*
(*Placement Art, a Beginner's Guide to Feng Shui*)

Ms. Lindsay makes a striking statement considering that *Torah* presents similar information regarding the direction of **North** as a most auspicious one:

*"…In the City of our God, in His holy mountain, beautiful in elevation… is Mount Zion on the sides of the **North**, the City of the great King."*
~ *Psalm 48:1-2*

*"The chamber which faces **North** is for the priests who have charge of the Altar…*
~ *Ezekiel 40:46*

*"He also brought the bronze altar which was before the Lord, from the front of the Temple… and put it on the **North** side of the new altar."*
~ *2ⁿᵈ Kings 16:14*

Meanwhile, most schools of *Feng Shui* agree that the direction of **South** represents the **Fire** element. From this account, we clearly see that God instructed Moses to place the Lampstand of **Fire**—the *Menorah*—on the **South** side of the Tabernacle.

A search of Scripture reveals a repeating pattern of the *Feng Shui* principles for placement that are in perfect harmony with the principles God ordained for His creation. He ensured the Law of *Feng Shui* would forever remain a part of His record. There is indeed a Master Plan for God's Divine Design:

*"Then David gave his son Solomon the **blueprints** for the entrance,*
its houses, its treasuries, its upper chambers, its inner room, the place
*of the mercy seat; and the **plans** for all that he had by the Spirit for*
the courts of the house of the Lord…"
~ *1st Chronicles 28:11-12*

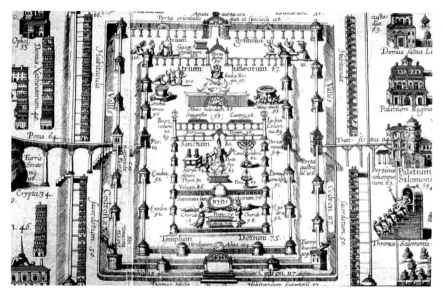

"Son of man (Ezekiel), describe the house…and let them (Israel)
*measure the pattern… Make known to them the **design** of the house*
*and its **arrangements**, its **exits** and **entrances**; its entire design and*
*all its ordinances, all its **forms** and all it laws. Write it down in their*
sight, so that they may keep its whole design and all its ordinances
*and perform them. This is the **Law of the Temple** [Feng Shui]."*
~ *Ezekiel 43:10-12*

To understand this Law of the Temple is to understand *Feng Shui*. It's simple and uncomplicated. I find it quite unnecessary to cloud the beauty of God's original natural laws with the superstitious myths that have evolved over the centuries to make *Feng Shui* complex and spiritually offensive to the more conservative-minded observer. There is a goodness that flows with the current of the breath of life. It blesses all who are in its path and leads them to *"recline in green pastures and beside still waters."* (Psalm 23:2)

Arranging furniture and architecture according to specific dimensions and *Feng Shui* principles is a recurring Biblical theme, beginning with the building of Noah's Ark:

> *"Make yourself an Ark…and this is how you shall make it: The length shall be 300 cubits, its width 50 cubits, and its height 30 cubits. You shall make a window and you shall…*
> *set a door in its side." (Mouth of Ch'i)*
> *~ Genesis Chapter 9*

When Moses was given the blueprints for the Tabernacle in the Wilderness (*Mishkan*), God instructed it also to be built in accordance with *Feng Shui:*

> *"Speak to the children of Israel to make Me a sanctuary that I may dwell among them. According to all that I show you, that is the **pattern** of the Tabernacle and the **pattern of all its furnishings,** so shall you make it."*
> *~ Exodus 25:8-9*

At the time King Solomon undertook the building of the original Temple in Jerusalem, he sought out the greatest minds in the world to help him accomplish this daunting task. It was clearly built according to specific measurements and incorporated all Five Elements of *Feng Shui*: **Wood, Metal, Fire, Earth and Water**. And upon its completion, as King Solomon pronounced a blessing over the Temple and the vibrational frequency of the musicians began to flow, it is recorded that the Glory of God's own Spirit fell from Heaven onto the people below. This was a manifestation of the perfect flow of God's breath of life (*ch'i*) moving through a sacred space, enhanced by *Feng Shui.*

*"Now the house which King Solomon Built was specifically **measured**...the house windows had beveled frames [Glass is **Water Element**; Beveled Produces refracted light – **Fire Element**]]. Against the wall of the house he built chambers of different shapes and sizes to support the beams [managing the flow of ch'i to work in concert with the Natural Law] ... The Doorway [mouth of ch'i] for the middle story was placed on the **right side** of the house [according to Feng Shui, the path to Helpful People, the Elders]... And Solomon built the inside walls of cedar board; from the floor to the ceiling he paneled with wood [**Wood element**] ... The inner sanctuary was overlaid with pure gold [**Metal Element**]... The description of the 'Wings of the Cherub' suggests the **Guardian** of the Inner Sanctuary [Guardians are used in Feng Shui for protection] ... There were costly stones in the floor and the great court was enclosed with hewn stones [**Earth Element**]... He made*

25

*pillars with 2 rows of pomegranates [Earth element of Feng Shui] ...
And he made the Sea of cast bronze **(Metal Element)**... containing
2,000 baths [**Water Element**]" ~ 1ˢᵗ Kings 7:1-26*

*"And when the trumpeters and singers were as one, to make one
sound [vibrational frequency] and praised the Lord...the house of
the Lord was filled with a cloud so that the priests could not
continue ministering, for the Glory of the Lord filled the Temple." ~
2ⁿᵈ Chronicles 5:13-14*

So what is the purpose in exact placement of furnishings,
windows, doors and other contents in our environment as was
accomplished in Solomon's Temple? According to *Feng Shui*, the
wind or *ch'i* that flows through our environment can nourish us or
deplete us, depending on its vibrational frequency. Encouraging the
flow of positive *ch'i* by directing its movement in conjunction with
natural law, your surroundings will enjoy a more uplifting, healthy
and inviting space. Conversely, if you collect clutter, overstuff a
room or block the fresh air from flowing through, your health and
mental well-being is likely to suffer. You may succumb to confusion
and feel stuck in stagnant space.

Clearing your clutter, arranging furniture so that it does not block
the pathway, and diffusing essential oils is a great way to enhance
your healthy flow of *ch'i*.

Chapter 6 –
The Hebrew-Chinese Connection

Let's examine some basic words and letters that will illustrate the relationship between pre-Exilic Hebrew as it was spoken prior to the prophet Ezra and Mandarin Chinese, the language of *Feng Shui.* Hebrew and Mandarin are both picture languages. It was during the Babylonian captivity of Israel that the original Hebrew word picture *aleph-bet* changed to Arabic characters.

There are many similarities between the vocabulary of *Feng Shui* and the ancient Hebraic rendering of the same words. For example, we've already established that the word *ch'i* literally means "the breath of life." It is more commonly referred to as "energy" or life force. The Hebrew expression, *cha'i,* also means "life." But in the original languages, there are no vowels — hence it is the same word for both.

Here is a table of other language pictures comparing Chinese *Feng Shui* terms to the earliest form of Hebrew letters for similar expressions:

Earth Element	Chinese Symbol for Earth	Hebrew Letter *Tav* (A Covenant Sign with Earth)
Water Element	Chinese Symbol for Water	Hebrew Letter *Mem* (Water)
Fire Element	Chinese Symbol for Fire	Hebrew Letter *Sheen* (A Consuming Fire)

There are other parallels between the Chinese and the ancient Hebrew traditions. For instance, China's <u>Monthly Ordinances</u> dating back to the 3rd Century B.C.E. included a canonical classic entitled, *The Record of Rites* or *Li Ch'i*. One of the rituals called for the "Son of Heaven" to perform the appropriate rituals. Compare these directives with the writings of the ancient Hebrew *Torah* regarding Israel's "Son of Heaven," *the High Priest*, dating back to the same period:

CHINESE (Taken from *Li Ch'i*)	HEBRAIC (Taken from *Torah*)
1. Appropriate monthly sacrifices	1. Appropriate monthly sacrifices (Lev. 1)
2. Proper ceremonial robes	2. Proper ceremonial robes (Lev. 16:4)
3. Eat appropriate foods	3. Eat appropriate foods (Lev. 11:1-47)
4. Perform proper ceremonies in the Hall of Light (*ming-t'ang*)	4. Perform ceremonies in the Hall of Light (Tabernacle with *Menorah*) Lev. 16:16-19
5. Promulgates instructions for tasks of agricultural season	5. Law for agricultural seasons. Gen. 8:22 Lev. 25:3-5 and 22
6. Uses Four seasons to frame the annual temporal cycles of the natural world	6. Four Seasons are established. Gen. 8:22 and Deut. 11:14; Psalm 104:19

The similarities between the pre-exilic Hebrew language and the Mandarin Chinese language are so remarkable that they suggest a fundamental link between these two great cultures. So what could be the explanation for these similarities? I believe the answer lies in the fact that 5,000 years ago, there was only one unified Earth Language. Most scholars agree that *Feng Shui* also dates back to this same time frame. It was during this period that a significant event in history occurred, forever linking all peoples, languages and cultures:

"Now the whole Earth had one language and one speech...And the Lord said, 'Indeed the people are one and they all have one language...So the Lord scattered them abroad from there over the face of all the earth and they ceased...[from their plot against God]. Therefore, its name is called Babel because the Lord confused the language of the whole Earth." ~ Genesis 11:1,5,8-9

Torah records this account of the Tower of Babel when all people on Planet Earth spoke the same language (approximately

5,000 years ago). Because of their wicked plot to overtake and dethrone the Creator, the fate of confusion and dispersion befell them. They attempted to defy God's order and natural law. But the interesting thing to note from this account is that before the scattering of the people, everyone knew the same things and spoke the same language. It is the opinion of this author that the similarities between the Chinese practice called *Feng Shui* and the *Torah* account of God's natural laws are the result of the Tower of Babel and its aftermath.

Tower of Babel

Chapter 7 –
Followers of "The Way"

The mystical side of **Feng Shui** is partially rooted in the spiritual philosophy of *Taoism* (or Daoism). *Tao* refers to religious traditions and concepts. These traditions have influenced East Asia for over two thousand years and some have spread internationally. The Chinese character *Tao* 道 means *"The Path"* or *"The Way."* In the Taoists' Cosmology (study of the Universe), *Tao* in its manifested state was the prime cause of the **yin and yang** or the Law of Opposites.

Chinese theology says the Supreme Being of *Tao* transformed as the **Three Pure Ones** before the incubation of the first man and woman. These Pure Ones are called:

"The Universally Honored One of Origin"
"The Universal **Lord of the Way** and its Virtue"
"The Universal Lord of the Numinous Treasure"
~ Wikipedia

I want to emphasize the 2nd manifestation of *Pure Ones* of Taoism, *"The Universal **Lord of the Way** and its Virtue"* because identical verbiage can be found in the ancient texts known as the Holy Scriptures:

*"And Thomas said to Him, 'Lord...how can we know **the way**?'*
*And Jesus said to him, "I am **the Way**, the Truth and the Life.*
No one comes to the Father except through Me."
~ John 14:5-6

31

*"...If he found any who were followers of **the Way**...he might bring them to Jerusalem.*
~ Book of Acts 9:2

"And Paul (Apostle) went into the synagogue...persuading concerning the Things of the Kingdom...But some did not believe, and spoke evil of **"The Way..."**
~ Book of Acts 19:8-9

"And about that time, there arose a great commotion about **"The Way."**
~ Book of Acts 19:23

"I (Apostle Paul) persecuted **this Way** *to the death..."*
~ Book of Acts 22:4

"But this I (Apostle Paul) confess to you, that according to **the Way**, *which they call a sect, so I worship the God of my fathers believing all things which are written by the Law and the Prophets."*
~ Book of Acts 24:14

"But when Felix heard these things, having more accurate knowledge of **the Way**, *he adjourned the proceedings..."*
~ Book of Acts 24:22

In a book entitled the *Tao Te Ching*, there are several spiritual directives very much akin to Judeo-Christian teachings. The Chinese translation of John's Gospel says that *"In the beginning was the **Tao** and the **Tao** was made flesh...*

Tao, a term translated as "The Way"; *Te* refers to "Virtue"; and *Ching* refers to "Laws." Thus the *Tao Te Ching* could be translated as *The Law of Virtue and Its Way*. This can also be said of the original Hebrew instructions, *Torah.*

C.S. Lewis in his book *"The Abolition of Man"* uses the word **Tao** to describe the **source of objective truth** in combating moral relativism. Is it possible that the One who said *"I am the Way (Tao), the Truth and the Life"* is in fact the 2nd manifestation of the Pure Ones? Indeed I believe He is One and the same!

Much like the Tower of Babel was a pivotal event in history that provides an explanation of how *Feng Shui* became a primarily Chinese practice, there is another historical event which I believe reveals the connection between *Taoism* and *Judeo-Christian* spiritual practices — an event that occurred 2,000 years ago—the same time that Chinese scholars attribute to the birth of *Taoism:*

*"Now when the Day of Shavuot (Pentecost) had fully come, they were gathered Together, all with one accord. And suddenly there came a sound (vibration) From heaven, as a rushing, mighty Wind (**Ch'i**)... and there appeared to them like tongues of **Fire**...and they all were filled with the Holy Spirit and began to speak with diverse tongues (languages) as the Spirit directed.*
*Now there were dwelling in Jerusalem, devout **Jews from every nation under heaven**. And when the sound occurred, the multitude...**heard them speak in each his own language**.*
*...This is what the Prophet Jo'el spoke: And it shall come to pass that I shall pour out of My Spirit on **all** flesh...And as David our father and prophet said...*
*'You have made known to me **the Way** (Tao) of life."*
~ Book of Acts Chapter 2

The history books record the presence of Jews from the Kaifeng Tribe in China dating to the 8th Century. And yet there is a monument there that suggests the Kaifeng Jews immigrated much earlier during the Warring States period approximately 2,000 years ago. This too lends credence that the principles of *"The Way"* called *Tao* may have

33

been brought to the great nation called China from that event in Jerusalem, since <u>every</u> nation under Heaven was represented on that day.

The origin of **Feng Shui** is intertwined with many threads woven through the pages of Hebrew History. All roads lead to the beginning, because *"In the beginning, God..."* The natural law of *Feng Shui* is the Creator's gift to the whole Earth to be nurtured and enjoyed.

Part 2 –
The Healing Arts
of Feng Shui

Chapter 8 –
The Heart Chakra

As I wrote in my book, *Scriptural Essence*, the Heart Chakra is the center stem on the body's *Menorah*. The *Menorah* in ancient texts refers to the Lampstand that stood on the Fire-side of the Temple in Jerusalem. The center lamp is called the *Shammash*, or the Servant lamp. It is the 4th Lamp, located exactly in the center of the *Menorah*. Similarly, the Heart Chakra is the 4th energy point along the spinal column.

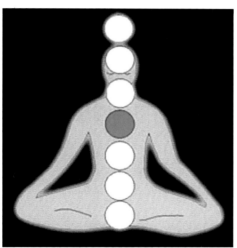 

The universal depiction of the Heart Chakra encompasses a Star of David or Mogen David. This is a six-sided design that has a very sacred meaning. In the center of the Mogen David is a Hebrew Dalet, which is the 4th letter of the alphabet and has a numerical value of 4. **Dalet means DOOR.**

This sacred geometric shape symbolically means, "**as above, so below**" in many languages and cultures. **The Double Mobius Star** (*Mogen David*) represents the Law of Polarity or Opposites: fire/water, masculine/feminine, heaven and earth. It is the symbol of perfect peace and balance between Heaven and Earth. The downward positioning triangle merges with the upward positioning triangle directly at the **heart center**. The descending triangle (points down) represents the creative, female, yang energy. The ascending triangle (points up) represents the male, yin energy. This symbolizes the two becoming one or *Echad,* in Hebrew. Similarly, it speaks of the macrocosm/microcosm — that which takes place on the earth plane also takes place in the realm of spirit.

This is significant because the "Door" is the *Mouth of Ch'i* in *Feng Shui*. When keeping the body, soul and spirit in harmony and balance with the Creator, access is made through the physical "*Mouth*

of Ch'i" or the Heart Chakra, **the Door.**

In the world of Energy Medicine, the chakra system is used as a litmus test as to the health of the body. The life force of the body, the *ch'i,* moves through the spinal column, and the energy points along the way are the seven chakras. The Heart is the gateway to the three chakras below, which ground us to the Earth and the three chakras above, which connect us to Heaven – another image of the Star of David.

As we learned from the origins of *"Tao,"* the 2nd of the **Three Pure Ones** is called *"The Lord of the Way."* Likewise, the historic record of Scripture reveals Yeshua (Jesus) in this same personology: *"And Jesus said to him, 'I am the Way, the Truth and the Life.'"* ~ *John 14:5-6*

Now, couple this revelation with the Heart Chakra and its center *Dalet* or **Door** and you have yet another picture of the Messiah Yeshua. The Heart Chakra with its center *Dalet* or **Door** is the gateway to all body systems. The identity of *"the Door"* is revealed as Yeshua (Jesus) in the ancient Scriptures:

> *"I am the Door. If anyone enters through Me,*
> *he will be saved and go in and out…"* ~ *John 10:9*

Today, the body is the Temple of the Holy Spirit. It is my belief that in balancing the *Temple Feng Shui,* you must first access the body's *ch'i* through the **Door,** which is the Heart Chakra. According to energy specialists, the Heart Chakra's element is Wind or *ch'i* and its pathway (*Tao*) is the emotion of **love**; the spirit of **praise;** and the sense of **touch.** When the Heart Chakra is weakened, it affects all three dimensions of the Temple — Body, Soul, and Spirit in the following ways:

- **Physical Dysfunctions (Body)** - heart conditions, asthma, lung & breast cancers, thoracic spine, pneumonia, upper back, shoulder problems

- **Mental and Emotional Issues (Soul)** - love, compassion, confidence, inspiration, hope, despair, hate, envy, fear, jealousy, anger, generosity

- **Spiritual (Spirit)** - forgiveness, unconditional love, letting go, trust, compassion

Chapter 9 –
Good Vibrations

The hectic and stressful lifestyles of the 21st Century contribute to poor health and premature aging. Thousands of Americans suffer from insomnia, worry and other stress-related dis-ease. *"Dis-ease"* actually means "not at ease" and is a word derived from the vibrational state of the body's natural energy operating at unhealthy levels. Just as the element of **Water** (H_2O) can exist in different states of vibration depending on temperature, our bodies also experience similar changes when the energy that surrounds us or moves through us vibrates at different temperatures.

Noted author and *Feng Shui* consultant, Karen Kingston, claims that life forms existing at the lowest astral or energy plane cannot survive beyond a certain vibrational level (*Clearing Clutter With Feng Shui*). For instance, cockroaches congregate at the lowest level of astral light. That's why they are so repulsive. Cockroaches usually cluster and thrive around filth, clutter and garbage. Think about the way you feel when you get near similar types of environments. You immediately want to run the other way and escape that sensation as quickly as possible. The reason for this feeling is the negative vibrational energy you experience when you are in those situations. You instinctively know it's bad for you. Conversely, have you ever discovered a cockroach in your home that was belly-up dead? Why? Because the energy vibration in that room was too high for the roach to survive.

Even the energy created by your thoughts and actions directly influence your health and well-being. Excessive stress, for example, is the result of energy vibrating internally at unhealthy levels. Stress can ignite the "fight or flight" mechanisms and exhaust the adrenal

41

system. If stress goes unbridled, it will eventually cause a breakdown in your mental and physical wellness. Understanding how *Feng Shui* can be employed to control stressful situations will empower you to eliminate this harmful energy within your environment.

Of course not all *dis-ease* is rooted in emotional and environmental stress; but like the cockroach, most *dis-ease* cannot thrive at the higher vibrational levels. *Dis-ease* in the body is often rectified through positive thought patterns and applying *Feng Shui* principles to enhance your energy. King Solomon wrote in his book of wisdom that *"A merry heart does good like a medicine"* and *"As a man thinks in his heart, so is he"* (Proverbs 17 and 23)

The Baby Boomer Generation is experiencing stress at a rate never conceived by our parents' generation, yet we seek simplistic answers to these complex problems. *Feng Shui* is a tool that provides simple, workable solutions to balance and harmonize every area of life by minimizing unhealthy energy and encouraging a more peaceful existence.

The Western pursuit of longevity while living life to its fullest has reached epidemic proportions. This Generation, which comprises the Baby Boom of the 1940's, rebelled against the societal norms of the 1960's and observed the changing of the Millennial Clock in 2000, is now obsessed with discovering the proverbial fountain of youth. The rise in alternative health and fitness centers, organic markets, cutting edge nutritionals, cosmetic surgery for every body part, and the Eco-Greening strategies for Planet Earth continue to skyrocket. Neighborhood Day Spas emerge overnight as we are driven to preserve our youth and beauty at any cost, thereby igniting the *Destructive* cycle of life called "stress."

By utilizing the principles of *Feng Shui*, we can create a sense of wellness and still maintain a haven of rest from the chaotic search for immortality. As humanity races to find *Shangri-la* and regain its youthful days gone by, it digs the grave of stress deeper and wider than ever. A return to a centered, balanced and peaceful coexistence with our environment provides the wellspring for magnificent aging. Growing older is not a bad thing! Aging with grace, health, and vitality is a beautiful, *Productive* cycle of life.

We only have to look at the amazing longevity of the people of *Torah* to see that well-being was a lifestyle. In the case of Moses, he lived 120 years with perfect vision and vitality to the very end. (Deuteronomy 34:7)

Setting healthy priorities is good *Feng Shui*. The placement of what is most important in life can make the difference between health and *dis-ease*, wealth and poverty, life and premature death. This is the age of electronic information. Everything comes to us at the speed of a "mouse click." If you need to speed it up, get a bigger modem! Examine your daily routine. How much time is set aside for work, for errands, for chauffeuring kids or attending their activities? What about meals (cooking and eating), bathing, dressing, personal grooming, housekeeping and laundry, and, and, and—and what else can you add to the list!

Do you work outside the home? Calculate your hours on the road commuting and at the workstation. Now assess how much time is apportioned to meditation; to relaxation; to leisure; to play and recreation. Oh, and how much of that schedule allows for sleep? Is the ratio just a little lopsided? Is the time you spend with your family really more like "Ships that pass in the night?" Do you enjoy your meals together, engaging in meaningful conversation? Or, is it in front of the television, eat and run, or not at all? Well, you'll have to be the judge of your personal priorities and what effect they have on your family and your overall well-being. But it might be worth a second look at how *Feng Shui* flows through your surroundings.

The Creator established a wonderful schedule that guarantees ample times of refreshing....

*"Six days shall work be done, but the seventh day is a Sabbath of solemn rest…You shall do no work on it; it is the **Rest of God** in all your dwellings." ~ Exodus 34:21*

Was this command of God to keep the Rest Day holy just a requirement to make people worship Him? Or was it, in fact, a gift that brings a remarkable and supernatural experience of revitalization, health, clarity of mind, renewed creativity and peace? If you observe the lives of the people of *Torah,* they were extremely prosperous, blessed with beautiful families and thrived for hundreds of years on the Earth. Is the seventh day "time-out" just some strange phenomenon that was for then and not for now? The answer is obvious. Examine your own life. How do you measure up against the standard? Consider taking one day in seven to <u>Rest</u> — not church hopping; watching football, or doing household chores. Enjoy the entire day promoting rest and rejuvenation of the Body, Mind and Spirit. Engage in activities that only nurture and support your well-being and peace of mind.

Televangelist Pat Robertson once told of his journey to accomplish a weekly Rest Day to decompress and get before God with the gloves off. That means, nothing in hand to substitute for your time with the Creator. At first it was nearly impossible, because the mind wants to move and talk and drive you crazy with "other things you should be doing." But if you persist, the shift will occur and you will find yourself accomplishing much more in the other six days than you could have imagined. And your stress levels will diminish.

Challenge yourself with "Good Vibrations" by making "Good Choices." Remember, <u>you</u> choose your schedule and <u>you</u> set your own priorities. So the ball is now in your court. Time to *Feng Shui* the Ball Court!

Feng Shui – God's way

Chapter 10 –
Musical Feng Shui

"And so it was that whenever the distressing spirit was upon Saul,
that David would take a harp and play it with his hand and Saul
would become refreshed and well and the distressing spirit
would depart from him."
~ 1ˢᵗ Samuel 16:23

It has been said that music is the satiating food for the soul and
the medicine that *soothes the savage breast*. Certainly, many famous
classics have stood the test of time because their melodious tones
evoke peace, joy and contentment in the human spirit. What attracts
people to music? Why is the music industry a multi-billion dollar a
year business? Music is played in stores to induce consumers to buy;
music is played in hospitals to encourage healing; music is played in
homes, in cars, on the heads of joggers, cyclists and boating
enthusiasts. Wherever we go, we take our favorite music with us...
Why?

Balancing the acoustics of life may be found in recent discoveries in the field of vibrational and tonal therapies. Sound waves and vibrations can have a profound effect on the human body. When the proper sound frequency is introduced, the environment can be positively enhanced — even the cellular structure of the body can be strengthened. Imagine how this type of *Feng Shui* might impact your health and well-being.

As early as 530 B.C.E., Greek Mathematician Pythagoras discovered the numerical ratios that determine the concordant intervals of the musical scale. In the late 1990's Dr. Leonard Horowitz and Dr. Joey Puleo discovered this ancient musical matrix encoded in the Bible —specifically in a book of the *Torah.* Beginning in Chapter 7, verse 12 of *Numbers,* this entire musical system is encoded in the Hebrew language. The musical tones are called the "Solfeggio" tones. Dr. Horowitz, a Jew who has traced his origins to King Solomon, believes the original musical sounds produced by the musicians in Solomon's Temple, which brought down the *Shekinah* glory from Heaven were these same Solfeggio tones.

He also believes that when recreated, the Solfeggio notes can effect vibrational healing in the body and the environment. I encourage you to read more of this fascinating study in Dr. Horowitz' book, **Healing Celebrations** (Tetrahedron Publishing Group).

Today we particularly remember Pythagoras for his famous geometry theorem. The sacred geometry that results from these healing vibrations and tones is now studied by leading scientists around the world.

Dr. Masaru Emoto conducted amazing research in Japan to observe the effects tones, music, prayers and verbal blessings have on water. Even polluted water molecules transformed into sacred geometry resembling the six-sided mobius Star of David when blessings and healing tones were applied:

The Solfeggio Frequencies in Water Crystals

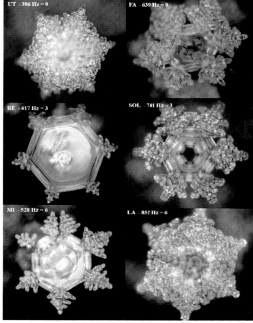

Today, many hospitals and healing centers employ the power of sound, especially music therapy to promote healing of the body, soul and spirit. And so, the story of the Israeli Shepherd boy David who played the psalms on his harp as King Saul was refreshed and restored to health takes on new meaning in the light of 21ˢᵗ Century science. The Universal Natural Laws of Creation contain many secrets that have been with us since the beginning of time. Now, we can apply these natural laws and unleash the power of health and prosperity that God has always desired for us to experience.

Chapter 11 –
The Essence of Feng Shui

The power and mystique of fragrance has captured the imagination of both men and women for centuries. The use of therapeutic essential oils is not a new concept, although most Americans are fairly new to the practice of applying them. In the days of Queen Hadassah (Esther) circa 400 B.C.E., it was a common practice for Persian women to prepare for their wedding by learning to apply essential oils. This course of study lasted up to one calendar year. The first six months of preparation were dedicated solely to learning all the different applications for the oil of Myrrh. *(Esther 2:12)*

Feng Shui God's Way takes its cue from the ancient masters. The prophet Isaiah referred to the oil trees in the land of Israel. *Yacov* (James), a disciple of Jesus, wrote that the elders should anoint the sick with oil and pray the prayer for healing. Essential oils are rich with healing properties. They are made from various flowers, leaves, bark, stalks, and growing plant life found everywhere on the Planet. Psalm 104 from the Bible speaks of the *"oil that makes your face shine"* and that the *"trees of the Lord are full of resin (oil)."* The value of essential oils, though lost during the Dark Ages, was highly esteemed in bygone eras and has re-emerged as the most powerful natural healing substance of the 21st century.

The historic roots of *Feng Shui* and the use of essential oils are woven through the pages of the *Torah* and other Hebraic writings as evidenced by *Feng Shui* experts. For instance, the ancient Jewish mystics developed a metaphysical book of philosophy called the *Kabbaláh*. This is the mystical element of Hebraic thought, discussing the origin of life. According to *Feng Shui* author, Jami Lin, *"To understand the basic tenets of* <u>Kabbalah</u> *is to understand the Tree of Life.* <u>Kabbalah</u> *states that the Original Force--God, the* **Divine Essence** *was and is good and whole…"* *(The Essence of Feng Shui)* And because the word for "Smell" and "Spirit" are identical in Hebrew—*Ruach*—Jews of antiquity also called God's Spirit, the *"Divine Essence."*

The Tree of Life as described in *Torah* was one of two trees encompassing the center of God's creation. The Tree of Life was the source for immortality. As we learned in Chapter 1, God prevented the original man and woman from accessing the Tree of Life because creation had been defiled through their disobedience, and the defilement must not be perpetuated.

Inasmuch as the sap and the leaves of many trees produce the essential oils used for healing and enlightenment, it is no surprise that the potential for ultimate life-giving immortality would come from the Biblical Tree of Life. And while the essential oil of this immortal Tree awaits its appointed time, the hope for its healing powers remains a future reality for all Believers. Hear the words of the prophecy:

"In the middle of the street, and on either side of the river, is the **Tree of Life**…*The* **leaves of the Tree are for the healing** *of the nations."*
~ Revelation 22:2

There are a number of informative books on the market explaining the various uses of essential oils, including the essences described in the ancient Hebrew texts. For more information on this subject, I recommend my own book *"Scriptural Essence—Temple Secrets Revealed,"* available at **WomanScents.com** along with the brilliant work of Dr. David Stewart, *"Healing Oils of the Bible,"* available at **AbundantHealth4U.com** and many other resources.

Regarding my choice for essential oils, the premiere Therapeutic Grade A oils are the Young Living Essential Oils. I believe these are the same quality as those used in the ancient Temple. These oils are also available through **WomanScents.com**

"And when Aaron lights the Menorah in the morning and at twilight, he shall diffuse sweet **Frankincense,** *a perpetual essence...."'*
~ *Exodus 30:7*

Enhancing your space with the "essence" of *Feng Shui* can be accomplished in a couple of different ways. I prefer diffusing the oils in each room to create a mood or to rid the air of dangerous toxic black mold, bacteria, viruses and foul odors. A cold-air diffuser is the best for therapeutic grade oils.

Another tool for your *Feng Shui* toolbox are essential oil spritzers. These are easy to use and very powerful in shifting the energy in a particular space.

In Part 3 of **Feng Shui, God's Way**, you will learn how I used oil spritzers in my *Feng Shui* practice to enhance and inspire sacred spaces.

Young Living Diffuser

Chapter 12 –
The Subliminal Power of Feng Shui

In *Feng Shui*, the Bagua Map or Grid as it is sometimes referred, identifies the major areas of human life within each section of an individual's environment. This environment can be a home, the property surrounding the home, an office building or each individual room within the design. The *Bagua* is our new Chinese term that originates from the Book of Changes called the *I Ching* (*Yee Jing*). *Bagua* is defined as a geometrical hexagon or 8-sided design of trigrams, based on an ancient Chinese binary system. Eight in the Hebrew Language represents *"New Beginnings"* and comparatively, the eight segments of the *Bagua* are considered to be the building blocks of the life. So life can begin anew each time the blueprint of *Bagua* is employed to arrange and rearrange the items in your environment. Like many of the Hebrew traditions handed down through the centuries, the Chinese have also adopted many traditions and incorporated them into the art of *Feng Shui.*

By now you know that energy or *ch'i* enters your space through the main entrance to the building. We call this the *Mouth of Ch'i.* Once inside the entrance, the natural flow of energy gravitates toward the various and distinctive parts of the home. Items like a staircase, a wall, a hallway, furniture, plants, or clutter can greatly influence where this natural energy flows. The different segments of the *Bagua* map are delineated into sections that correspond to the important issues of life: Health and Family; Children and Creativity; Marriage and Relationships; Fame and Reputation; Wealth and Prosperity; Travel and Helpful People (Mentors); Knowledge and Self-Development; and Career and Business. By learning to skillfully orchestrate the items you place in your environment, you will find that corresponding elements of your lifestyle will also be enhanced. If a particular area is not in line with God's natural laws of *Feng Shui*, that area of the person's life may also be out of balance.

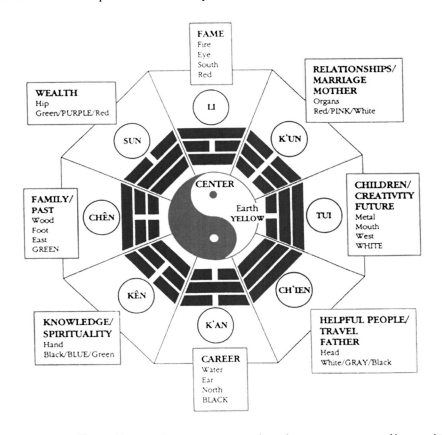

I recall a client whose teenage daughter was struggling with compliance and attitude toward her family. This lovely girl had once been the picture of youthful exuberance and joy. Her dream of becoming a ballerina high on her list of goals was suddenly dashed as her parents watched a total transformation into the world of the "Gothic" dark side. Her mother pleaded, begged, cajoled, bribed and tried every tact she could imagine to coax her daughter to reject this new lifestyle. The entire family was affected by her bizarre behavior and angry outbursts.

When I arrived at the home to do a *Feng Shui* assessment of the situation, the mother took me on tour to see and to "sense" what might be going on in the environment that could possibly cause the dramatic change. Nothing seemed out of place. It was a lovely home, and the woman herself had an intuitive sense of how things should be arranged—most women do! But as we approached her daughter's bedroom, the mother forewarned me that the room was sort of "creepy" and she herself loathed to even go inside.

Upon entering the child's room, I sensed a foreboding presence — an almost evil energy. It didn't take long to discern the source of this "*shar ch'i*." The entire wall overshadowing her bed was filled with pictures of monsters, gargoyles, wizards, witches and evil grimacing faces. The center of the wall boasted a large poster of a bizarre and evil-looking wizard, depicted as though waving his magic wand ominously over the pillows on her bed. Having learned of the subliminal and suggestive power of artwork while attending the *Western School of Feng Shui*, I knew immediately that this display of negative *ch'i* was having a major influence on the young girl.

I decided to interview her and engage her help in resolving the matter. The girl, whom I will call Jennifer (not her real name, of course), was reticent at first, but soon relaxed into the interview with great curiosity. I asked her about her choice of wall décor and how she felt when residing in her room. She claimed to like it, although her words lacked real enthusiasm. Further inquiry revealed however, that it was not really her first choice – it actually began with a mistake — an error made in a local poster shop.

A few months earlier, Jennifer was eager to find a poster of a beautiful ballerina to display over her bed. She found the ideal poster at a shop nearby and brought it home in the conventional poster tube. But to her dismay, upon opening the tube, it was not the picture of the beautiful ballerina, but the startling face of the evil-eyed wizard. The poster had been mistakenly loaded into the tube labeled "Ballerina."

Jennifer intended to return the *Wizard* to the poster shop in exchange for the one she really wanted. However, time passed and she procrastinated as so many of us do. One day she came across the poster again, stuffed at the back of her closet. Jennifer looked at it for a few moments and decided to hang it in her room, rather than return it for exchange. After all, she thought, "What could it hurt?"

It didn't take long for the influence of the negative *ch'i*, breathing down upon her in sleep every night before Jennifer began to gravitate to the "dark side." From that one poster, she added many others—all of similar energy and negative messages and phrases. By the time I arrived on scene, the entire wall was virtually covered with abysmal artwork.

So, I challenged Jennifer to participate in an experiment with me. I explained that I was on a special *Feng Shui* assignment to see if changing artwork and room decorations would make a difference in how people felt about themselves. Engaging her in this way was just the right ticket to receive her cooperation, rather than her resistance. Jennifer agreed to remove all the pictures for one week, putting them in storage so they could not be viewed. We set an appointment to meet again and assess any changes that may have occurred.

Upon my return to the home one week later, I was astonished to be greeted by this beautiful young girl with a glistening smile and shining eyes. It was Jennifer! There was no need to ask further questions — I had my answer, and so had she. With great joy and enthusiasm, Jennifer shared that she was sleeping more peacefully and didn't feel depressed or tired anymore. As the week drew to a close, Jennifer already knew of the terrible error she'd made in not returning the *Wizard* immediately. For her, this was a great lesson in procrastination! She excitedly told me that earlier that morning, her

mother had taken her to an art gallery and found an oil painting of a prima ballerina, framed in antique gold filigree – her reward for participating in our *Feng Shui* experiment.

Jennifer's story reminds me of the writings of one my favorite spiritual mentors, the Apostle Paul:

"Whatever things are noble and true; whatever things are just and pure; whatever things are lovely and give good report; if there is any virtue and if it is praiseworthy — then meditate on these things. The things which you have learned and have seen in me, do these things and the God of all Peace will be with you always."
~ Philippians 4:8-9

Part 3 –

The Practical Fruits of Feng Shui

Chapter 13 –
Furniture, A Moving Experience

Now that you understand the origin of *Feng Shui* is seeded in the roots of Creation, it's time to apply the Natural Law of *Wind and Water* to your life. In order to satisfy your natural curiosity and logical thought processes, we will approach this part of *Feng Shui God's Way,* from a practical perspective.

It's quite probable that you have experienced the sensation of entering a room, a building or other space and instinctively knew that something was amiss. It just didn't "feel" right. An assessment of the situation suggested everything was in order, but you were not at all comfortable. Although it may not have been readily apparent, there was a probable cause for the discomfort you were experiencing. More than likely a violation of *Feng Shui* principles was taking place, but you were not equipped to recognize it. For instance, according to *Feng Shui*, any items of furniture blocking the direct route of energy coming through the entrance to the room will usually create a cool, unfriendly environment. Perhaps the chairs were arranged in a negative fashion. Seating arrangements should never be positioned in such a way that visitors have to sit with their backs to the entrance of the room. Why? The unconscious concern about what's happening behind them brings an uncomfortable sensation as though they must constantly be looking over their shoulders. Have you ever wondered where we acquired the Western expression of "Watch Your Back?" There is a foreboding sense of fear that stems from *unseen* potential danger.

I want to tell you my own personal experience with unfriendly furniture placement. It all began with a lifelong dream for a house with bay windows. Since I was five-years-old, my fantasy carried me to places of enchantment--especially cottages and bungalows with beautifully enhanced tri-corner bays and pillow-laden window seats. When my husband Joe and I decided to build a new home, my mind immediately started the process of bringing the dream to reality. I carefully planned how I would appoint and arrange everything in this magnificent room with bay windows. I purchased a tuxedo sofa and two wing back chairs to create a "nook" setting. The wing-backs were strategically positioned in the corners of the bay with a round table separating the two chairs. The sofa was used as a room divider between the formal dining area and the living room. The final step was to place a beautiful cherry wood table behind this elegant sofa to further offset the space. What a picture of Western splendor: Victorian essence with a hint of *Anne of Green Gables*. My fantasy room was complete. Of course, I knew nothing of *Feng Shui* and its sacred taboos for furniture placement, but I knew this room would be the envy of all my guests. Much to my chagrin, a strange pattern began to emerge that would soon prove me wrong.

One by one, the guests would arrive for parties, dinners and drop-in socials. Friends would stop by just to say hello, but no one would sit in my special room! Predictably, they would gravitate to the less-exciting family room adjoining the kitchen with worn furniture and well-traveled carpets. I was disheartened and perplexed. "Doesn't anyone else see the glory of this fantasy room?"

Sometime later, while cooling my heels in a doctor's office, I read a magazine article about *Feng Shui,* defined as the "Chinese Art of Placement." The article said people do not like to be situated in such a way that someone could sneak up from behind. The article went on to say that *Feng Shui* principles govern our environment for good or for bad. When these principles are violated, negative patterns develop in the lives of those within that environment. People become uncomfortable, depressed, even ill. Then I saw it! My carefully placed tuxedo sofa put my visitors in a compromising—almost foreboding position. I was still skeptical of this *Feng Shui* notion, but

I had to find out for myself if there was any truth to it. Inquiring minds do want to know!

I returned home and planned my new strategy. Even if it meant sacrificing the theme of Green Gables, I had to find out if what I'd read was true. The game plan was set in motion. I paid a visit to the local bookstore to learn more about furniture placement and *Feng Shui*.

My first obstacle was learning to pronounce "Fung Schway" clearly enough to communicate to the desk clerk just what it was I was looking for! You can imagine my embarrassment when I asked to see a book on "Fegn Shooey!" I quickly learned that my feeble attempt at phonetic Chinese was failing miserably. The sales clerk very graciously responded, "Our *'Fung Schway'* section is over on the left." Ugh! The crimson blush in my face told anyone who was looking that I had just experienced my first *Feng Shui Faux Paux* !

The number of *Feng Shui* titles was a little overwhelming, but I finally selected a book on clearing clutter. After devouring the information at break-neck speed (I was beginning to feel desperate), I set my mind to test the power of *Feng Shui*.

The "room in question" was purposely rearranged to ensure that every person who might sit there could see the entrance to that room. I also hung mirrors to provide expanded views and present the illusion that the outside landscape was coming through the bay window. I moved the artwork and downsized the table arrangements to provide a more auspicious, less-cluttered feel to the entire space. What a difference! But the real test was how my friends and family would "feel" when they entered. I am happy to report that my initial encounter with *Feng Shui* was a complete success! Everyone raved about my special room, asking, "What have you done differently? Is this new furniture? Did you get new drapes?" They couldn't quite put their finger on what had really happened, but now the room welcomes and invites them in. The conclusion I learned is that people instinctively behave according to *Feng Shui* principles without even realizing it. Their own energy responds to the surrounding environment and causes them to naturally gravitate toward the more positive, healthy flow, or shy away from the more negative *ch'i.*

Okay, now you have an idea of how placement may affect the way you feel and even think. So, let's look at another area of *Feng Shui* that directly influences your energy level. Consider how it makes you feel whenever you clean out an area of your home that's long overdue for a check-up. While growing up in Indiana, my family practiced an end-of-winter ritual called "spring cleaning." I learned much later in life that this tradition comes from the practice of clearing the "leaven" from the home during the Jewish feast of Unleavened Bread. As a child I dreaded this annual observance, but had to admit that everything felt great after the work was finished. It was invigorating to clear away the cobwebs, scrub the walls, wash the windows and disinfect the cupboards. The whole house seemed to come alive with renewed energy. Little did Mom realize she was practicing *Feng Shui* as she directed this ritualistic operation.

There is a special kind of vitality that flows through a clean, clutter-free environment, much like spring cleaning breathes new life into a winter-worn house. When you apply the principles of *Feng*

Shui God's Way, you can have that spring-clean feel all year long!

Still Skeptical? Consider this: You don't have to believe in or even understand the *Law of Gravity* for it to work. Whatever goes UP must come DOWN. The results you get are already determined by the natural forces governing the circumstances. When you apply the governing Law of Gravity, the outcome is foreseeable. All of God's natural laws work predictably. These immutable processes are innate to Planet Earth's life cycles and operate automatically. If you violate a natural law, if you swim upstream against the current of life's flow, then you will reap a negative consequence. Conversely, when you go with the flow, blessings follow.

Feng Shui, when applied according to natural law, will predictably bring forth renewed energy and the potential for great blessing. My husband Joe calls this the "**GMH**" Theory; that is, **God Made it Happen**! As you learned in Part I, *Feng Shui* is a natural law of creation set in motion by God and will continue to operate as long as the Earth remains.

Chapter 14 –
Clutter Kills

Living in the most progressive and prosperous nation on the Planet stretches our natural habitats to unnatural limits. The American Dream tells us we are entitled to a home of our own. And when we get that home, we promptly fill every nook and cranny with treasures, keepsakes, mementos and general all-around clutter! It's as if we subconsciously increase our collection of "things" so we can later justify a bigger place to store them! How many times have you said, "We need a bigger house!"

In addition to our regular everyday clutter, we specialize in collectibles: vintage newspapers, antique porcelain, salt & pepper shakers, silver spoons and so it goes. What about you? Has your home become the great gathering place for collectible clutter? Are your countertops piled high with magazines, mail, school papers, memorabilia, old photographs, scrapbook collections and knick-knacks from days gone by? Oh, and what about your closets? Are you clinging to fashions that no longer fit? Perhaps you are maintaining a wardrobe of every size you've worn in the last 10 years? What about mending? Has your fix and repair pile grown to epidemic proportions?

Of course, you may be among the more elite collectors. You know, the pink pigs, red roosters, purple cows and green unicorns. Let's not forget those dolls: Cabbage Patches, Tickle Me Elmos, Barbies, Beanie Babies, Story Books, G.I. Joes, Madame Alexanders and Pokemons. The more sophisticated doll collectors gravitate to the QVC and Home Shoppers' Network high-profile dolls created by their favorite celebrities.

If you are numbered among the more conventional collectors,

you probably invest in stamps, coins, baseball cards, matchbox cars and train sets. But the connoisseurs of art collect Lennox, Hummels, Lladros, Salvatore Dalis and Thomas Kincaids. If you can conceive of it, Americans can collect it! Let's face it, collecting is part and parcel of being American.

Some people are more dedicated collectors than others, but each of us has amassed little treasures at one time or another. Clutter can even become part of our identities. I recall the story of a woman referred to as the "Angel Lady." She had collected over 1,000 angels and proudly displayed each one in her cramped little abode. What amazed me was the number of hours she expended maintaining them! The angel collection became her life's work.

The most vivid personal example of collectible clutter came through our friends, Lance and Linda. They asked my husband and me to help relocate the contents of their two-story 3,500 square foot house to a recently purchased one story, two-bedroom bungalow. I'll never forget the challenge that presented itself on that blistering June day in Phoenix, Arizona: "How do you squeeze the contents of Buckingham Palace into Tinkerbell's summer cottage?"

And while that question still resonated in our brains, an even more ominous challenge awaited us at the top of the stairs. "Oh, no! It couldn't be! Not that! Not eight cast iron potbelly stoves! God forbid! No American home should be without them – especially when the house has no chimney! Now this is SERIOUS Clutter Collecting.

No one escapes the web of clutter. We are all victims of it-- especially the members of the Baby Boomer Generation. Doting parents who survived the Great Depression indulged us "Boomers."

These indomitable people put their lives on hold to fight World War II. And when the war was over, they were determined their children would never want for anything! They coddled a generation of children who eventually rebelled against convention, raising their voices in defiance of authority. The volatile 1960's evidenced the beginning of America's pursuit of self-indulgence. As the Baby Boomers aged, this pattern of self-indulgence took the form of faster cars, bigger houses, recreational vehicles, cabin cruisers and 4-wheel-drive play toys.

The art of collecting evolved into something much bigger than a mere pastime. The Boomers discovered retro-collecting. Antiques! Historical clutter! From coast to coast and border to border, antique stores and garage sales offer unlimited opportunities to buy other people's clutter. It's not that we haven't enough clutter of our own, but the passion for collecting drives us onward.

Today, clutter maintenance equally competes for our time and energy, as do family, work and recreation. With the maintenance of clutter comes the complex problem of "Where do we put it all?" Not to worry! A new phenomenon has emerged in recent years--storage rental units. Part of America's income now goes to pay rent for clutter storage – the stuff that never gets used or enjoyed, only stored. It's all part of your "just in case" collection. "My WHAT collection?" You know, the just-in-case-I-might-need-them-someday tools and gadgets that collect in the junk drawer. There's a proverbial saying in America that goes something like this: "The minute I throw it away, that's when I'll need it." The truth is that you can create that need by expecting it to come. The *Law of Expectation* (another Universal Natural Law) predicts that if you truly believe every item discarded will soon be needed, it then becomes a self-fulfilling prophecy. Your thought energy will vibrate at that level of expectancy and eventually the circumstance will arise. Why not ask yourself how many times you've needed it in the past and then expect THAT same result in the future. If you are hanging on to something "just in case," you probably don't need it after all and are now free to move it out of your space.

I live in an upper-middle-class suburban development where every house is equipped with a three-car garage; and yet at any given time of the day or night, the driveways are cluttered with one or more vehicles. Why? You guessed it! The garage is no longer available to accommodate the family's transportation. Its new assignment is "clutter storage." But look at the bright side: If your garage is big enough to store all your "stuff," then you won't have to pay for clutter storage rental!

How do you break the clutter cycle when it's so engrained in our culture? Begin by making an intention to deal with each item when you first pick it up. Decide whether it's really needed in your life and then put it away, discard it or recycle it. You'll save energy and your home will breathe a lot easier.

What about the collection of gifts from friends and loved ones? Gift clutter comes wrapped in festive paper, shiny ribbon and a compelling sense of obligation to keep and display it. "Aunt Sarah may come over! What do I tell her if the peacock cookie jar she gave me is not proudly displayed on my kitchen counter?" Who cares that you don't even like cookies or that you already have two other cookie jars from Aunt Mary and Grandma Phelps! Ah, but they have both passed on so at least you don't have to worry about them dropping in to find their gifts are not in use! You're keeping this clutter as a memorial! Adopt a healthy new philosophy: It really is okay to not love every gift that is given you! With grateful appreciation, pass it on to someone who really likes it.

Speaking of memorials, most American homes are cluttered with gifts displayed out of guilt or shrines erected in memory of departed loved ones. Have you ever stopped to think about the emotional and spiritual energy that's generated by memorial clutter? When attachment to a material object is rooted in your attachment to a deceased loved one, it can be extremely unhealthy--mentally, emotionally and spiritually. In many instances, the cycle of grief really never ends because the object that once belonged to the dearly departed now steals energy from you! If you allow it, clutter will call to you from the grave. Hanging on to these objects will sap your strength and may even hinder your ability to move forward with your life. Stop and ask yourself how you feel when you see Mom's knitting needles or Dad's pipe. Do you feel warm and uplifted or sad and mournful because Mom and Dad are no longer around to use them? You may even feel guilty for not spending more time with them when they were alive. For many, hanging on to clutter from those relationships temporarily soothes these anguishing emotions, but it's almost impossible to think about an item associated with someone who's passed on and not think about death. Death is the great thief. It steals the breath of life from those we love. It's difficult to argue that keeping remembrances of death is healthy. Once the grief process is past, it's time to look ahead.

The Jewish custom today is to conduct burial within 24 hours of the passing, unless a Sabbath falls during that period. The family then expresses mourning through a custom known as "sitting shiva," a ritual lasting seven days (aish.com). The headstone is not even placed until the one-year anniversary of the passing (JewishMonuments.com). Life moves forward, never forgetting, but never regretting. *Feng Shui, God's Way* teaches *"There is a time to be born, and a time to die...A time to weep, and a time to laugh...A time to mourn, and a time to dance."* (Ecclesiastes 3) The poet Henry Wadsworth Longfellow understood the significance of the "letting go" process when he wrote:

"Look not mournfully into the past. It comes not back again. Wisely, improve the present. For it is thine."

Similarly, the Amish communities handle death in the same manner in which they live their lives – quietly and simply. I recall

73

one sunny afternoon in early October some years ago, my sister Barbara and I visited an Amish community in Northern Indiana. As we rode in a turn-of-the-century wagon to the outer edge of the property, our tour guide directed our attention to a potter's field located just across the creek bed. To the curious onlooker, it resembled rows and rows of wooden stakes neatly aligned in perfect formation. It was not unlike the pattern of the cornfields we had passed a little earlier – a place of perfect harmony and balance. The guide explained that upon the passing of a community member, a grave is prepared in this field immediately next to the last member of the community who passed on. A wooden cross is then carved and a number is engraved on the cross, the next number in succession. The family and friends never visit the gravesite, because they literally believe a Scripture passage that says, *"We walk by faith, not by sight. We are confident rather that to be absent from the body, we're present with the Lord."* (2 Corinthians 5:7-8). For them, there is no more earthly attachment to that body – only the blessed hope of eternal reunion with the loved one in Heaven. And God's incredible peace seems to blanket that Amish household like a thick, flannel covering on a chilly evening. Though sorrow sometimes lingers in the night, that wonderful joy does come in the light of day.

Compare the Amish philosophy with the practice of most Americans: costly funeral expenses; mournful gatherings at the mortuary; burial plots that require perpetual maintenance. The grieving process for mainstream America is often prolonged through weekly visitations to the gravesite, followed by a need to adorn the site with flowers, pictures, memorabilia, ornaments—or sadly, storing the ashes of the dearly departed in the home. While driving by a cemetery last winter, I actually observed a family decorating a burial site with a Christmas tree, garland, tinsel, bulbs and bows. It was quite sad to realize that their attachment was still so strong. Unresolved grief will clutter your very soul. Mourning should not last too long, lest it steal your own breath of life.

Feng Shui God's Way tells us that, "*Weeping may last all night, but in the morning there is joy*" (Psalm 30:5) and that, "*I would have lost heart unless I had believed that I would see the goodness of the Lord in the land of the living.*" (Psalm 27:13) There are goals to be set, appointments to keep and dreams to dream. Always remember that your life is a gift from God, too precious to let fall by the wayside of regrets and sorrows.

The process of separating yourself from clutter is a very personal and sometimes traumatic experience. But when you understand the positive benefits of *Feng Shui God's Way*, it will help you to take that first step to downsize your environment for the sake of your health and happiness. Remember the goal of *Feng Shui* is to promote free-flowing energy to every area of your life. Stagnant, dead energy produces stagnant, dead results.

Each person must make the journey of de-cluttering alone. No one else can make these decisions for you. Only you can live with yourself, "post clutter." Hold tight to the vision of the life you desire and that God desires for you. It's a life free from entanglements and relics of the past. It's a world of peace and simplicity; an environment of perfect balance and harmony between you and your Creator.

When you begin to deal with your clutter, don't rush the process. Think about the reasons you have kept each item. Hold it in your hand and ask yourself, "Does this drain me emotionally or hinder my spiritual growth? Do I truly feel good about keeping it?"

And WHY am I keeping it? One thing is certain: your relationship to your possessions will either renew your strength or sap your energy. It can generate joy or foster depression and guilt. Keep in mind that every item that shares your environment with you requires energy. Your "stuff" is just energy vibrating at different levels. Remember that with every item of clutter comes maintenance through dusting, storing, moving or repairing. And even when you are not consciously thinking about your clutter, your subconscious mind will think about it for you. It will watch over your clutter all night long like a sentry standing guard over his possessions. At the end of the day when you should rest and re-energize for the challenges of tomorrow, your subconscious mind is busy tending to your clutter. From there, your clutter collects mentally. In the back of your mind, you're always thinking about the garage that needs to be cleaned or the closet, or the pantry, or the basement or the storage shed. There's never enough time to manage your clutter, so your subconscious mind will manage it for you.

Freeing yourself from the bondage of clutter will not solve the world's problems, but I guarantee you that removing excess baggage from your environment will bring life-giving energy in greater measure. This concept holds true with all your possessions. Think of how your computer hard drive becomes sluggish when too many files are stored in its limited disk space. And what about your own body? How's the plumbing? *Feng Shui* those pipes and keep them clean and uncluttered!

Ridding your life of stagnant, energy-stealing clutter will enable you to reap tremendous benefits. You will not only be amazed at the results, but you will be motivated to do more. *Feng Shui God's Way* is a life free from entanglements, clutter and stagnation. Decide now to enjoy clutter-free living. Make your intention clear. Set your sights on total liberty in every area. Remember the words of the ancient and wise Rabbi:

"Take heed and beware of covetousness, for your life does not consist in the abundance of the things you possess."
~ Luke 12:15

Chapter 15 –
My Feng Shui Coloring Book

The vibrational frequency of Color will change the frequency of everything it touches. Imagine if creation was only in black and white! What a depressing view of life we would see. But in His glorious design, the Creator infused the brilliance of Color with all its magnificent shades and energetic tones into the whole of creation.

The renowned naturalist, Dr. Stanley Burroughs, wrote of the healing power of Color in his classic work *"Healing for the Age of Enlightenment."* Similar to the frequency of Sound, the Colors of the light spectrum vibrate at different levels and actually create the all-too-familiar pattern of the Star of David. As we saw in Chapter 10, Dr. Emoto's depiction of clustered water crystals was in the form of a six-sided geometric design. Similarly, Dr. Burroughs' mathematical expression of the light spectrum is remarkably similar.

When choosing colors for your home, consider the universally accepted *Feng Shui* Color Spectrum because of its frequency effect on human emotion and behavioral patterns. The Color Spectrum of the *Bagua* provides direction for each compartment of our lives. Here are a few ideas from the *Bagua:*

Red — The Fire Element; Fame and Reputation — Stimulates and dominates. Red reduces the size of rooms and increases the size of objects. It's great as an accent color, but not suitable for dining rooms, children's bedrooms, kitchens or workshops. Emotionally, Red is associated with anger, shame and hatred.

Yellow — The Earth Element; The Center of the Home — Associated with enlightenment and intellect. Yellow stimulates the brain and aids in digestion. Its qualities are optimism, reason and decisiveness. Its negative side is craftiness, exaggeration and rigidity. Yellow is suitable for hallways and kitchens, but not for meditation rooms or bathrooms.

Green — The Wood Element; Health and Family — Symbolizes growth, fertility and harmony. Green is restful and refreshing. Its positive associations are optimism, freedom and balance; its negative side is envy and deceit. Green is great for therapy rooms, conservatories and bathrooms. Green is not recommended for family rooms, playrooms or Studies.

Blue — The Wood Element; New Knowledge — Peaceful and soothing and is linked with spirituality, contemplation, mystery and patience. Blue's positive associations are trust, faithfulness and stability. Its negatives include suspicion and melancholia. Blue can be used in meditation rooms, bedrooms, therapy rooms and as a means of enlarging spaces. Not recommended for family rooms, dining rooms and Studies.

Purple — The Wood Element; Wealth/Prosperity — Encourages vitality. Purple is impressive, dignified and spiritual. Positive associations are excitement, passion and motivation. Its negatives are mournfulness and force. Purple is great *Feng Shui* for bedrooms and meditation rooms, but not bathrooms or kitchens.

White — The Metal Element; Creativity and Children — Symbolizes new beginnings, purity and innocence. Its positive qualities are cleanliness and freshness; its negatives are cold, lifelessness, starkness and clinical. Use for bathrooms and kitchens, but not for children's rooms and dining rooms.

Black — The Water Element and Your Career — Mysterious and Independent. Use carefully on walls. Black is best applied as an Accent Color. Its positive qualities are intrigue, strength and allure; its negatives are death, darkness and evil. Black should not be used in teenagers' rooms, therapy or living rooms.

Silver or Grey — The Metal Element; Helpful People and Travel; Synchronicity — Not a good color for wide wall space. Better used as accent and to balance the elements.

Pink — The Fire Element; Love and Relationship—Associated with purity of thought and has the positive association of happiness and romance, with no negatives. Suitable for bedrooms and children! Not suitable for kitchens or bathrooms.

Orange — The Fire Element; Powerful and Cheery. Orange encourages communication. Its positive qualities are happiness, concentration and intellect; its negative side is Rebellion — Keep orange out of your teenager's room! Orange walls in prison cells have created rebellious outbreaks. Orange can be used in living rooms, dining rooms and hallways in small doses. Avoid using Orange in small rooms and bedrooms.

Brown — The Earth Element; Suggests stability and weight. Its positives are safety and elegance; its negatives are dinginess, depression and aging. Good for studies (dens), but not for bedrooms or BABY BOOMERS!

Beware of Peach — Using the color Peach in your bedroom is asking for trouble! There is a Chinese idiom that refers to "Peach Blossom Luck." It means "a spouse with a "roving eye." Peach in the bedroom is perceived to have the potential to entice married couples into adultery." ~ *Practical Encyclopedia of Feng Shui, p. 74*

Now be creative! Select your colors wisely and with *Feng Shui* in mind. Try coloring therapies on a smaller scale to see the effects. Then move on to bigger projects. ENJOY!

Chapter 16 –
Feng Shui at Home

Are you ready to implement the Universal Law of *Wind and Water* throughout your home, room by room? The first step is to orient the *Bagua*. For simplicity, I've chosen the following Grid that has been converted to a square, rather than the traditional octagonal design. Orientation is more easily accomplished for Western architecture using this Matrix form. Now, I want you to envision your home floor plan overlaid by the Grid and imagine at what point the *ch'i* enters and the different directions it can travel throughout your environment. Missing pieces to your floor plan, such as an L-shaped home will create or a Recessed Entryway will affect the true location of each sector. Refer to the *Western Guide to Feng Shui* for more information on this.

WEALTH & PROSPERITY "Gratitude" REAR LEFT Wood Blues, purples, & reds	FAME & REPUTATION "Integrity" REAR MIDDLE Fire Reds	LOVE & MARRIAGE "Receptivity" REAR RIGHT Earth Reds, Pinks, & whites
HEALTH & FAMILY "Strength" MIDDLE LEFT Wood Blues & Greens	CENTER "Earth" Yellow & earth tones	CREATIVITY & CHILDREN "Joy" MIDDLE RIGHT Metal White & Pastels
KNOWLEDGE & SELF-CULTIVATION "Stillness" FRONT LEFT Earth Black, blues, & greens	CAREER "Depth" FRONT MIDDLE Water Black & dark tones	HELPFUL PEOPLE & TRAVEL "Synchronicity" FRONT RIGHT Metal White, gray & black

When you enter through the front door, the *Mouth of Ch'i,* the location of that door relative to the center of your home is consequential. This is how you determine the flow of energy into your life. For instance, if the front door is in the middle of the house, energy enters through the **Business and Career Section**. If the door is to the left of center, then energy comes through the **Knowledge and Self-Development area.** And should the front door be right of center, *ch'i* enters by way of the **Mentors, Elders and Travel Section**.

The areas that most people want to enhance are **Love and Relationships**, **Business,** and **Wealth and Prosperity**. If your front door enters about Center of the building, then you are entering through your Career/Business section. The Love and Relationship sector is always in the far right corner of the home, with Wealth and Prosperity in the far left corner. I will not go into extensive detail or instruction on how to completely orient your home and office *Feng Shui*, but just to provide you some helpful insights which should produce favorable and noticeable results rather quickly. For a more in-depth understanding of *Feng Shui,* I highly recommend *The Western Guide to Feng Shui* by my personal mentor and teacher, Terah Kathryn Collins. After attending as many classes as my local community offered; and after reading a dozen books on the subject; I chose Terah Collins' philosophy and her form school of *Essential Feng Shui* to expand my understanding of God's Law of Wind and Water. It works best for Western architecture and lifestyles. Okay, let's begin….

Entryway or Foyer ~ If the *Mouth of Ch'i* is centered at the front of your home, then you are entering through the Career and Business Sector. Black accents are appropriate here because the color Black represents the water element and nourishes business energy. A water feature or small fountain works well in this area if there is ample room. Remember, however, that space is sacred and not to be cluttered.

Oil Spritzer ~ Essential Oil of Cedarwood. The scent of Cedar evokes an image of a room containing **many doors that open into passageways** leading to your heart's desire. Spray your closet with

Cedarwood if you have moths. You can also use Cedarwood to spray your plants if they have insects. Cedarwood enables a steady flow of energy throughout the home. ~ *Vibrational Healing with Essential Oils by Deborah Eidson.* (Young Living Cedarwood is Item #3509 – Available at **WomanScents.com**)

Affirmation ~ *"I welcome life and the goodness that God brings to me each morning. My confidence is in Him and all that He wants to accomplish through me this day."*

The Master Bedroom ~ NO MIRRORS! If you use large mirrors, move them to the inside of the closet door so they can be closed off or to the Master Bathroom. Mirrors are too high energy for restful sleep and often interfere with personal intimacy - despite what you may have seen in the movies!

Feng Shui God's Way ~

The two primary purposes for this room are **Rest and intimacy**. So fashion the room with items that speak to those subjects. That means no workout equipment; no computers; no televisions or electronics; no work piled high in the corner or on the nightstand. It also means no family photos. These create a subliminal message that the people you love are "watching" what you do!

If you live alone and like it that way, then one (1) nightstand is sufficient. But if you are married or desire a lasting, loving commitment of marriage, then two (2) nightstands at the same height are critical. When nightstands are the same height, there is no subliminal message that one partner is or will be "over" the other. It is an equitable relationship. Colors that work in the Master Suite are luscious purples and mauves, rich blue-greens, and warm tones — but remember, no Peach. Create the feeling of "nesting" and warmth.

Rest is encouraged in every way. Artwork should be peaceful, elegant and romantic. If you are a married woman or a woman who wants to be married, refrain from pictures of single women, that is, one woman only.

Oil Spritzer For Romance ~ **Joy Blend** from Young Living. A rich, seductive aroma comprised of botanicals made for love: Rose, Jasmine; Ylang Ylang, Rosewood and more. The blend has been used for decades to help abate depression and nourish the spirit. The electrical frequency of **Joy Blend** is **188 MHz**, one of the highest of all essential oil blends. ~ *People's Desk Reference 2000* (Young Living Item # 3372 available at **WomanScents.com**)

Oil Spritzer For Relaxation ~ **St. Maries Lavender Oil** from Young Living. This exquisite therapeutic distillation is head and shoulders above all other lavender oils. The herb is grown organically on the Young Living Lavender Farms in St. Maries, Idaho, where the plants are carefully nurtured and cultivated, and oil lovers bless the plants with love energy. St. Maries Lavender is great for winding down before bedtime, yet its balancing properties can boost stamina and energy by day. The electrical frequency of **St. Maries Lavender** is **120 MHz.** (Young Living Item #3576 available at **WomanScents.com**)

Affirmation: ~ *"I am loved and I give love with great joy. All that surrounds me is beautiful and calm. The passion of life flows through me at eventide. I am at peace with God and His Creation."*

Home Office ~ The Color Red is most auspicious for the home office and signifies Fame and Reputation. Ideally, you will locate your home office in the corresponding sector of the *Bagua* Grid. If you are in a home-based business, some key factors to employ include Artwork that conveys positive messages that are very appropriate to your Business, Career and personal Achievement. Pictures which display uplifting phrases like "Leadership" or "Success" or "Opportunity" bode well here. If possible, your desk should **face the entrance to the room**, rather than toward the wall. But if this is not possible, then strategically place a mirror somewhere in your line of view so that you can see the doorway (*Mouth of Ch'i*) while seated at your desk. This relieves you of the subliminal stress of someone sneaking up from behind.

A water feature is also good *Feng Shui* for the Home Office. Water is an element which transmits Wealth energy. Remember the power of *Mayim Hayim* or Living Water from the *Torah*. It keeps you from stagnating in your business.

Your window view can also play an important role in *Feng Shui*. Ideally, having a healthy, mature tree growing outside the office window facilitates peace and harmony and allows your mind to manage the stress of doing business. But you must also be careful to manage your daydreaming! Corporations that are in the *Feng Shui* "know" ensure their Executive Suites are fully equipped with windows and scenic views.

Oil Spritzer ~ **Abundance Blend** from Young Living. This blend of rich, aromatic spice oils is often called the *Law of Attraction* in a bottle. In business, your goal is to attract all good things. Abundance Blend synergistically combines therapeutic grade Myrrh, Cinnamon, Frankincense, Patchouly, Orange, Clove, Ginger and

Spruce essential oils and attracts success like moths to a flame! The electrical frequency of **Abundance Blend** is **78 MHz**. *~ People's Desk Reference, 2000* (Young Living Item #3300. Available at **WomanScents.com**)

Feng Shui God's Way ~

The electrical frequency of **Abundance Blend** is equal to the frequency of the Universal *Law of Attraction*. When Einstein's Law of Vibration and Attraction was calculated mathematically, it resonated at a frequency of **78 MHz**—the same as Abundance Blend. All of God's Universal Laws work in synchronicity, one to another, creating harmony and balance. Challenge yourself with this amazing aroma to see what you might attract into your life!

<u>Affirmation</u> ~ *"I am grateful for all God has given me. My success and prosperity flow from His never-ending bounty. May all creatures great and small benefit from the abilities and talents bestowed on me from Above. I continually prosper and walk in health even as my soul prospers."*

Living Room Or Great Room ~ Warm and inviting is the ticket here. This is the place for family, activities and guests. Be mindful of furniture placement. Cozy corner groupings that do not block the healthy flow of *ch'i* were made for this Great Room. Remember the "back side" of furniture that may create a feeling of foreboding danger. If you must place a couch with its back to the entrance to the room, place a sofa table behind it with nurturing and supporting items. This reduces the stress.

Balance your elements with color, shapes and tangible expressions of the five elements. For instance, you may substitute the actual element with a representation of that element. We've already seen how a water feature like a table fountain can represent the water

86

element and bring wealth energy to the home office. A Red pillow or other accents in the Red Color Spectrum introduce the Fire element into this space, but too much Red can stir excessive high energy. *Feng Shui* is all about balance.

Oil Spritzer ~ **Purification Blend** from Young Living. Purification's powerful anti-bacterial, sanitizing properties cleanse and purify the air in this high-energy space. Its fragrance is fresh and clean. This is a blend of therapeutic grade Citronella, Lemongrass, Rosemary, Tea Tree, Lavandin and Myrtle oils that combine naturally to remove foul odors, add oxygen to the air and all without chemicals! The frequency of **Purification Blend** is **46 MHz**. ~ *People's Desk Reference, 2000* (Young Living Item # 3399 Available at **WomanScents.com**)

Affirmation ~ *"I bless this space with love and friendship. Our hearts are filled with joy because of the many kindnesses that are extended to us here and the kindnesses we are able to extend to others. We are a family—a community of caring, friendly people with integrity, pure hearts and good intentions."*

Balancing all areas with the five elements can be a challenge at times, but one well worth the effort. Discover your own intuitive sense of harmonizing the energy throughout your home, your office and your many sacred spaces. To assist you in the journey, here are some ideas to incorporate into your *Feng Shui* development. Mix and match; integrate some of your favorite things; rid the stuck spaces of old energy and items you no longer love or use. Have fun!

Earth Element (Genesis 1:1) ~ Yellow and Earth tone color spectrum; adobe, brick and tile; ceramics and earthenware; Artwork depicting earthy scenarios, deserts, outdoors. The "90-degree Angle" shape, i.e. squares, rectangles and flat surfaces.

Water Element (Genesis 1:2) ~ The Black and dark-tone spectrum of colors including charcoal and Navy or Midnight blue; reflective surfaces like glass and mirrors; actual water features like fish aquariums, table fountains, goldfish bowls, etc. Artwork that depicts waterfalls, lakes, streams, oceans or items heavy in the water element; the "Asymmetrical" shape, i.e. wavy, curvy, and free flowing.

Fire Element (Genesis 1:3) ~ The Red spectrum of colors; all indoor and outdoor lighting, candles, natural sunlight, fireplaces (even if no fire is lit); items made from animals, e.g. fur, leather, wool; Pets and wildlife; artwork that depicts people or animals, sunshine and fire; the "Conical" shape, i.e. triangles, pyramids, cones.

Metal Element (Genesis 2:12) ~ White and Pastel color spectrum; metal items, stainless steel, copper, gold, silver, aluminum, etc. Rocks and stones are considered in the family of Metal; crystals and gems; Artwork that depicts any of these expressions; the "Circular" shape, i.e. circles, ovals and arches.

Wood Element (Genesis 1:11) ~ The colors Green and Blue; Wooden furniture and objects; Floral printed upholstery and draperies; Art that depicts landscapes, gardens, flowers, and trees; the indoor plants, flowers and trees—including silk, which is a natural fiber; the "Columnar" shape, i.e. pedestals, poles, beams and stripes.

Feng Shui God's Way ~

To introduce the Wood Element, I do not recommend plastic flowers, because they are not alive; they are synthetic and petro-chemical in composition. I also do not recommend dried flowers, because they are **DEAD**! The life force or the *Ch'i* is gone. It's dead energy, and it will stagnate the frequency in this space.

Work with all the Elements in their various representations to balance your environment, room by room. You will find that even little changes can make a big difference. I find that Color is a powerful expression of energy. It can balance or be overbearing, so follow your sense of intuition. Consider a new home where all the walls are white. White represents the Metal Element. Add to that, a Kitchen with white or almond appliances; a white sink, and lots of chrome. All of these are Metal and the room will feel clinical or cold. This is a great opportunity to employ your *Feng Shui* tools to bring balance and harmony into the new space. Your family and friends will love it — and so will you!

These are just a few ideas to assist you in changing the direction of your life to a more joyous, fruitful and prosperous one. Even if you are skeptical at first, challenge yourself to try one or two concepts and see how it feels to you. You may be wonderfully surprised!

Feng Shui God's Way ~

A word of caution! **Go slowly and deliberately.** A little change can bring big results. I once had a client who, against my counsel, immediately implemented all 10 suggestions I provided. Eventually, all her desired outcomes came to pass, but not before utter chaos and confusion and heartache broke out! Remember that God's wonderful flow of energy is intended to bless and enliven the creation. Take care to nurture and appreciate that flow of life-giving *ch'i,* balanced with grace and love, to create harmony, joy and peace inside your world and His.

Feng Shui Quilt

"The Garden of Wind & Water"

Created by Barbara Kellogg
Barbara's Story Quilts © 2002
BarbaraManatee1@hotmail.com

Chapter 17 –
Final Thoughts...

Our journey together to discover **Feng Shui God's Way** has come to a close. It is my hope that this information has released the Spirit in you to boldly go where you have not given yourself permission to travel before. The secrets to life enhancement will most likely be found outside the proverbial "Comfort Zone." The so-called Comfort Zone is only perceived as Comfortable; but in reality, it's the *Stagnant* Zone, where life-giving energy has no place to flow and grow. It means you wither on the vine of life; and like the frog in the boiling water, you are oblivious to your demise. No frog in its right mind would jump into boiling water! But a frog could be "comfortable" in tepid or cool water, even if it sits atop a burner or flame. And because the ever-increasing temperature of the water is gradual, the frog is unaware how quickly he dehydrates on the road to death. If you find yourself stuck in any of life's wonderful pathways, be it health, career, leisure or relationships, then you are in a Comfort Zone that is heating up to uncomfortable outcomes. This is your time to *"step out of the boat and walk upon the water"* as the Apostle Peter did so long ago.

The Natural Law of *Wind and Water* was given by the Creator to work in concert with the Creation to help it flourish and grow. It has always been God's desire for His children to *"prosper and be in health even as our souls prosper."* (3rd John 2) But ignorance is a means to perishing. If we are unaware of the many tools and gifts that are available to us, we cannot benefit from them. **Feng Shui God's Way** is a tool to nurture and support you as you make healthy changes in your life and experience the joy of the boundless blessings that result from them. May God bless you and keep you and make

His face shine upon you.

Now, go and share the joy of *Feng Shui God's Way—It Was Here all the Time.*

THE BEGINNING